T0414021

TOOLS FOR CAREGIVERS

- **F&P LEVEL:** C
- **WORD COUNT:** 36
- **CURRICULUM CONNECTIONS:** animals, habitats, nature

Skills to Teach

- **HIGH-FREQUENCY WORDS:** a, ball, has, in, into, is, it, no, the, up
- **CONTENT WORDS:** claws, digs, eats, fox, good, hedgehog, hunts, keep, night, oh, quills, rolls, safe, sleeps, wakes, woods
- **PUNCTUATION:** exclamation points, periods
- **WORD STUDY:** compound word (*hedgehog*); digraph /qu/ (*quills*); /k/, spelled *c* (*claws*); long /e/, spelled *ea* (*eats*); long /e/, spelled *ee* (*keep, sleeps*)
- **TEXT TYPE:** information report

Before Reading Activities

- Read the title and give a simple statement of the main idea.
- Have students "walk" through the book and talk about what they see in the pictures.
- Introduce new vocabulary by having students predict the first letter and locate the word in the text.
- Discuss any unfamiliar concepts that are in the text.

After Reading Activities

Explain to readers that a hedgehog rolls into a ball to protect itself when it is in danger. Its sharp quills protect it from animals, like foxes, that try to bite or eat it. What other animal defenses can readers think of, like claws, shells, spikes, or stingers? If they could each have one, what would it be, and why? Have each reader share their answer.

Tadpole Books are published by Jump!, 5357 Penn Avenue South, Minneapolis, MN 55419, www.jumplibrary.com

Editor: Jenna Gleisner **Designer:** Emma Almgren-Bersie

Photo Credits: feedough/iStock, cover; Sergey Galushko/Dreamstime, 1; galdzer/iStock, 2tl, 10; Nevena1987/iStock, 2tr, 11; IrinaK/Shutterstock, 2ml, 12–13; Martina_L/iStock, 2mr, 8–9; imageBROKER/Alamy, 2bl, 14–15; Anne Coatesy/iStock, 2br, 4–5; supakrit tirayasupasin/Shutterstock, 3; BIOSPHOTO/Alamy, 6–7; Kuttelvaserova Stuchelova/Shutterstock, 16.

Library of Congress Cataloging-in-Publication Data
Names: Brandle, Marie, 1989- author.
Title: Hedgehogs / by Marie Brandle.
Description: Minneapolis, MN: Jump!, Inc., (2024)
Series: My first animal books | Includes index.
Audience: Ages 3–6
Identifiers: LCCN 2022054038 (print)
LCCN 2022054039 (ebook)
ISBN 9798885246613 (hardcover)
ISBN 9798885246620 (paperback)
ISBN 9798885246637 (ebook)
Subjects: LCSH: Hedgehogs—Juvenile literature.
Classification: LCC QL737.E753 B73 2024 (print)
LCC QL737.E753 (ebook) | DDC 599.33/2—dc23/eng/20221110
LC record available at https://lccn.loc.gov/2022054038
LC ebook record available at https://lccn.loc.gov/2022054039

MY FIRST ANIMAL BOOKS

HEDGEHOGS

by Marie Brandle

TABLE OF CONTENTS

WORDS TO KNOW

claws

digs

eats

quills

sleeps

woods

HEDGEHOGS

A hedgehog wakes up.

It is in the woods.

Oh, no!

A fox hunts.

The hedgehog rolls into a ball.

Quills keep it safe.

It has claws.

It digs.

It eats.

It sleeps.

Good night!

LET'S REVIEW!

What is this hedgehog doing?

INDEX